CLASS SCHEDU

MW00901104

Name _____   School _____

MONDAY	Time	Subject	Room

TUESDAY	Time	Subject	Room

WEDNESDAY	Time	Subject	Room

THURSDAY	Time	Subject	Room

FRIDAY	Time	Subject	Room

Made in the USA
Monee, IL
20 November 2020